A HUSBAND'S LITTLE BLACK BOOK

A
HUSBAND'S LITTLE
BLACK BOOK

Common Sense, Wit
and Wisdom For A
Better Marriage

Robert J. Ackerman, Ph.D.

Health Communications, Inc.®
Deerfield Beach, Florida

Publisher: Health Communications, Inc.
            3201 S.W. 15th Street
            Deerfield Beach, Florida 33442-8190

Cover photo and design by
Andrea Perrine Brower

To My Parents,
Who Have Been Married
For More Than 50 Years.

Introduction

After I said, "I do," I said, "What do I do?" Marriage licenses don't come with instructions. It wouldn't matter anyway. Most men I know don't read directions. That's why we can't program the VCR. After all, we secretly know that "Real men don't need directions." We would rather drive around for hours looking for our destination than ask for directions.

This book represents the collective wisdom I have heard over the years from both husbands and wives about what makes a good husband. It is not intended to teach you how to redo your life. It is about the everyday things that make living with her better. I hope you enjoy reading it and that it makes you think about her. It is the little things we do that make the biggest difference. Enjoy each other!

*Shampoo her hair
for her birthday.*

Don't eat potato chips in bed.

Put the toilet seat down.

Men always want to be

a woman's first love;

women have a more subtle

instinct: what they like

is to be a man's

last romance.

—*Unknown*

*Don't take more
out of your relationship
than you put in.*

Send her flowers on

an ordinary day.

Pains do not hold a marriage together. It is threads, hundreds of tiny threads which sew people together through the years. That's what makes a marriage last—more than passion or even sex.

— *Simone Signoret*

If she wrecks the car,
ask her if she is all right
before you ask about
the car.

Delete

"I told you so" from

your vocabulary.

Write down her telephone messages correctly.

Go grocery shopping with her.

Do the

grocery shopping

yourself.

Buy the holiday and birthday cards you send to your parents.

Marriage is our last,

best chance to grow up.

—Joseph Barth

*Don't give her advice
unless she asks for it.*

*Listen when
she talks about
her friends.*

*Look through her
high school yearbook.*

*Then in the marriage
union, the independence of
the husband and the wife
will be equal, their
dependence mutal, and their
obligations reciprocal.*

—Lucretia Mott

*Take her to bed
and just hold her.*

One of the best things

about marriage is

that it gets young people

to bed at a decent hour.

—M. M. Musselman

*Be honest, but
don't tell her things that
might hurt her feelings.*

Share the last

bottle of soda.

A woman is the only thing that I am afraid of that I know will not hurt me.

— Abraham Lincoln

*If you win
the game you're playing,
don't gloat.*

Past relationships
are better left in
the past.

*Let there be spaces in
your togetherness.*

—*Kahlil Gibran*

Do the laundry — and don't mix the whites with the darks.

Start a fire in the fireplace on cold winter nights.

*Love does not consist
in gazing at each other,
but in looking together
in the same direction.*

—Antoine de Saint-Exupéry

Take her away overnight

without the kids.

Take turns taking the children to the doctor's office when they are sick.

Don't put your wife on a pedestal; she doesn't want to be that far away.

When you're lost, stop and ask for directions.

*I can live for two months
on a good compliment.*

—Mark Twain

Give her praise.

Talk to her calmly.

Don't bring up her old boyfriends.

Rudeness is

the weak man's imitation

of strength.

—Eric Hoffer

*Call her in the middle
of the day just to say,
"Hello."*

Talk with her when you're worried about money.

Help her put her clothes back on. Many people will help you take your clothes off, but only a few will help you put them back on.

Find a moment alone with her on New Year's Eve.

A handful of patience is worth more than a bushel of brains.

—*Dutch proverb*

Learn to argue fairly. Don't use phrases that begin with "You always," or "You never."

If you feel empty when she's away, tell her when she gets back.

A bull does not enjoy fame

in two herds.

—*Rhodesian proverb*

Remember, she married you

so don't ask her to be logical!

Discuss your childrens' requests with your wife before you give them an answer.

Remember that arguments have three sides—his, hers and the facts.

*Do you want to be happy or
do you want to be right?*

Don't say anything about her weight gain and she won't say anything about your hair loss.

The test of a man or woman's breeding is how they behave in a quarrel.

—George Bernard Shaw

Marriage requires you to create many definitions of love.

Give her neck rubs when she comes home from work.

If she can't start the lawn mower, blame it on the mower.

Fill up the empty ice cube tray.

When I was young, I kissed my first woman and smoked my first cigarette on the same day. Believe me, never since have I wasted any more time on tobacco.

—Arturo Toscanini

A husband's silence often says more than we think. It is better to explain ourselves.

Clean your own fish when you go fishing.

Any married man should forget his mistakes —no use two people remembering the same thing.

—Duane Dewel

Keep her secrets.

Go car shopping together.

Be faithful, and remember,
it doesn't matter where you
get your appetite as long as
you eat at home.

Bake chocolate chip cookies together on a Sunday afternoon.

Loneliness and the feeling of

being unwanted is

the most terrible poverty.

—Mother Teresa

Take her to the park and push her on the swing.

She's your partner, so stand up for her.

Learn to cook three

different dinners.

*Men always talk about
the most important things to
perfect strangers.*

—G. K. Chesterton

*If you want to know
what's inside of her,
listen to what she says
and she will unfold.*

He has a right to criticize,

who has a heart to help.

—*Abraham Lincoln*

If you go away, give her the

telephone number

where you can be reached.

The most important thing a father can do for his children is to love their mother.

—Theodore Hesburgh

*If you forget her birthday,
have a good excuse. If you
forget your anniversary—
move out of town!*

Just think of all her unmentionables hanging in the bathroom as tools hanging in the garage.

Never go into her purse

unless she tells you to.

Flirt with her once in a while.

Where you used to be, there is
a hole in the world, which
I find myself constantly walking
around in the daytime, and
falling into at night.
I miss you like hell.

—Edna St. Vincent Millay

It is more important to go together than it is to know where you are going.

Don't hate, it's too big a burden to bear.

—Martin Luther King, Jr.

Order something for her from the Victoria's Secret catalog.

She has many needs,

but the most important

is to be needed.

Don't spend a lot of money

without talking it over

with her first.

If you find yourself
getting angry with her,
just walk away
for a while.

Turn off the football game during Thanksgiving dinner.

If the phone rings when you are making love, don't answer it. Who could be more important?

When there is nothing left to be said sometimes a hug goes a long way.

Take a lot of family pictures and arrange them in a photo album.

Surprise her by cleaning the house while she is gone.

*Don't rush her when
she's telling you a story.*

Love her for who she is,

not for what you would

like her to be.

See everything; overlook a great deal; correct a little.

—*Pope John* XXIII

The greatest danger to marriage is apathy.

While she is in the shower,

warm her bath towel

in the dryer.

*Fill the bathtub with
hot water and bubble bath
for her, light a candle, fill
a glass of white wine —then
leave her alone.*

Some things might not be

a big deal to you,

but they are to her.

Respect her feelings.

Marriage 101

Today's lesson is priorities:

Wife, children, job.

Wife, children, job.

Wife, children, job.

Any questions?

If listening to another person

is an art, become an artist.

Write her a love letter, but be careful about what you promise. You don't want to be guilty of male fraud.

*Sometimes you will get
the last words,
but they might be
"Yes, dear."*

Address
(one name only)

Her Name:
Work Address:

Work Phone:
Birthday:
Wedding Anniversary:
Anniversary Of First Date:

Favorite Color:
Favorite Song:
Favorite Flowers:
Favorite Perfume:
Favorite Restaurant:
Favorite Vacation Spot:
Favorite Side Of The Bed:

Dress Size:	*Blouse Size:*
Shoe Size:	*Pants Size:*
Stocking Size:	*Nightgown Size:*
Coat Size:	*Underwear Size:*

Also by
Robert J. Ackerman, Ph.D.

Silent Sons

Perfect Daughters

Children Of Alcoholics

Too Old To Cry

Abused No More

Let Go And Grow

Recovery Resource Guide

Growing In The Shadow

About the author

Robert J. Ackerman, Ph.D., is the husband of Kimberly Roth Ackerman, the father of three children and professor of sociology at Indiana University of Pennsylvania. And he tries to keep his life in that order.